BRIGHT ANGLES

Witty Solutions and
How to Spark Them

Daniel A. Maher

ISBN: 978-0-646-72770-7

"Glorious – a high-density protein bar of great ideas!"

— Rory Sutherland
Vice Chairman, Ogilvy UK; author of *Alchemy*

Table of Contents

Introduction: The Cupboard and Magnets   1

Chapter 1: Shifting Views   5

Chapter 2: Hidden Keys   11

Chapter 3: Halving Problems   17

Chapter 4: Oddball to Obvious   23

Chapter 5: Happy Accidents   29

Chapter 6: Magic Combos   35

Chapter 7: Forward Backward   41

Chapter 8: Animal Rescue   47

Chapter 9: Riveting Pivoting   53

Chapter 10: Re-Angling   63

Chapter 11: Curve Busting   69

Chapter 12: Wrong Angles   77

Chapter 13: Sparking   81

Over to You   89

Appendix: *The Bright Angler's Field Guide*   91

Quirky Quotes   105

Dedications   107

Author Bio   109

Introduction

The Cupboard and Magnets

I can trace my fascination with clever fixes back to a cupboard door in our family kitchen.

I was about nine years old, watching my father crouched under the sink, trying to repair a drooping door that wouldn't quite close. My dad was my hero, an engineer, entrepreneur, university lecturer, but also the kind of person who could build shelving units, tile a floor, or fix almost anything. To me, he could solve everything. Except that day, the door just wouldn't cooperate.

I don't know where the thought came from, but I piped up: "Dad, what about magnets?" Dad paused, looked at me, and then laughed. "That's brilliant! Why didn't I think of that? Nice one son."

It was a small moment, but it stuck with me. Not because I was particularly clever, but because it showed me something important: that sometimes a solution doesn't need to be complicated, it just needs a different angle.

That spark never really left me. Over the years I became a bit of an idea nerd. (Okay, when I say a bit, I should probably have said a complete and total idea nerd). Trust me, I could easily blabber until the blind concussed cows come home about fascinating solutions I've come across, whether from my own experience, or from history, nature, sport, space... wherever. And that's probably (err, definitely) one of the reasons why I wrote this book.

What I've learned, both in life and through my career, managing teams across hospitality, education, corporate offices, and innovation teams in both the public and private sectors, as well as mentoring entrepreneurs, is that ingenuity often comes from the simplest shifts in perspective.

And that's what this book is about: the joy of bright angles. They're reminders that clever solutions can come from anywhere, and from anyone. Which is why I'll be taking you through an eclectic mix of witty, wild, famous, obscure and peculiar examples of bright angles from around the world and through time. I've also sprinkled in a few from my own career which I felt were worth sharing.

But this book isn't just a collection of curious stories, I'll also share my thoughts on what sparks bright angles and some recommendations for how anyone, including business leaders who want to inspire their teams, can create the conditions for them.

The truth is, as cheesy as it sounds, I really wrote this book to inspire others. My hope is that this roller coaster tour of bright angles from all angles will not only captivate and entertain you but also ignite your own spark.

Instructions: How to use this book

This book is an inanimate object. Why do I point that out? Well, it's not going to monitor how you read it. It won't tap you on the shoulder if you skip ahead, and it won't sulk if you use it to swat mosquitos... *(eBook version excepted)*.

I say this because people often feel like they must "follow the rules" when they pick up a book. Not this one. You can dip in and out, skim, re-read, or binge cover to cover, whatever floats your book. Also, the last pages are deliberately blank in case you wanted to jot down some notes, hair-brained schemes, moon-shot ideas or back-of-the-envelope style eureka moments.

The only thing I'd suggest is this: when reading the examples, try to pause now and then, scratch your chin and think to yourself... how could this type of bright angle apply to my own circumstance.

And if you're the kind of reader who likes a shortcut, or a nudge when you're stuck, you'll find a special appendix at the back: *the Bright Angler's Field Guide.* It's a set of checklists you can flip to whenever you're staring at a blank page, shaping a half-formed idea, or trying to spark a team that's run out of fizz. Think of it as your bright-angle first-aid kit.

Okay, let's get into it. Enjoy the tour!

Chapter 1
Shifting Views

Some bright angles don't come from fixing what's broken. They come from changing the *way* people think and see things. A shift in perspective can turn the ordinary into something valuable, and the overlooked into something people suddenly want.

The Seating Fix
One of my favorite bright angles from my own career happened in a restaurant I managed years ago.

Like a lot of places, this one had a balcony with a view, and everyone wanted to sit there. The problem was, once the balcony filled up, the rest of the restaurant sat half-empty. Perfectly good tables near the bar or tucked into corners were treated like second-class seats. We ended up with long queues, frustrated customers, and staff under pressure to rush people through the "good" section, while other tables sat untouched.

It bugged me. Not just because it caused unnecessary stress, but because it felt like such a waste.

So, with the team, we tried a little experiment. We gave those "second-class seats" their own VIP makeover. Nothing too fancy, just some indoor plants, a few lamps, comfier chairs, (all from one Ikea shopping trip... shhh). Then we gave them new names: The Cozy Nook, The Green Lounge. And then... wham-bam... what do you know! People started requesting to sit at those tables. Queues moved faster. The pressure lifted. Revenue went up.

It's one of my favorites because it taught me something meaningful: ingenuity doesn't always mean inventing something new. Sometimes it's just about changing how people see what's already there.

The Same Map
I'm not sure when I first learned about this next one, but when I did, I thought it was fascinating. If you've ever been on an underground metro, and let's face it, you probably have, you'd instantly recognize the map. Those neat, colored lines,

the equally spaced stations, the way it all looks so clean and simple.

But here's the surprising bit: the famous London Underground map wasn't designed by a cartographer or a qualified designer, it was drawn up in the 1930s by a man named Harry Beck, who was an electrical draftsman. And once you know that, it kind of makes perfect sense.

Look closely at a metro map and you'll start to notice how it resembles an electrical circuit board, colored parallel wires, 90- and 45- degree angles, clear symbols. That was Beck's inspiration. Before his version, the Tube map was a confusing tangle of geographic accuracy: meandering tracks, rivers drawn to scale, streets overlaying the routes. Useless for commuters who just wanted to know where to get on and off.

Beck's version stripped all that away. Geography became irrelevant underground, no one cared what was overhead. What mattered was clarity. At first, officials thought it was too simple, but passengers loved it. The map became the standard, not only in London but in cities across the world.

Just like the restaurant fix, Beck's map didn't change the system itself. But it changed how people *saw* the system, and that made all the difference.

Water Walls

Sometimes shifting a view means placing things in clear view.

Traditional road warnings, flashing lights, bold signage, even hanging barriers, can all fade into background noise. Drivers get used to them, or worse, assume they don't apply. The result? Accidents that should have been avoided.

Thankfully, some witty engineers came up with a striking solution: a sensor triggered sheet of falling water stretched across the road with a glowing "STOP" sign projected onto it. The effect is dramatic, arresting, and unforgettable. Drivers might ignore a sign on a pole, but no one barrels through a wall of water with a red warning blazing across it.

This bright angle proved especially useful in warning trucks that ignored tunnel height restrictions, cutting incidents by nearly a third when first introduced.

Outer View

Sometimes it's the unexpected customers' view that triggers bright angles. Take the origin of the tea bag for instance.

Legend has it that in the early 1900s, a tea merchant named Thomas Sullivan began sending samples in little silk bags. The idea was that buyers would cut them open and brew the leaves as usual. But the instructions weren't always clear. So instead of fussing with scissors, some customers simply dunked the entire bag in hot water. What might have been confusion quickly became convenience A small misinterpretation turned packaging into product, and the tea bag habit spread until it became the default for much of the world.

So, what's the takeaway from this chapter? The facts may be fixed, but your angle isn't. Shift it, and new opportunities come into view.

Chapter 2
Hidden Keys

Ever spent ages looking for your glasses only to realize they were on your head the whole time? (It's ok, you can be honest, things like that happen to me all the time too.) I once drove home because I thought I'd forgotten my car keys... yeah, let that sink in.

Anyway, moving on.

That's the spirit of this chapter. Some bright angles are simply about noticing what's already there, right under your nose, and realizing it's the missing key.

Data Next Door

Ok so here's an example from when I managed a training academy for a global auditing organisation. Our courses focused on international standards, how to interpret them, implement them, and prepare for the inevitable audits. The big question was always: how do we find the right clients at the right time?

For a while, it felt like guesswork. We marketed broadly, hoping to catch the attention of organizations that might be interested. But then I noticed something almost embarrassingly obvious: the team who sat on the opposite side of the office from us, the audit planning team.

Their job? To schedule clients' audits. In other words, they had the perfect trigger points for our training. Pre-audit clients needed help to get ready. Post-audit clients often needed support to fix the gaps revealed.

Once that clicked, the cogs began to turn. By simply aligning our outreach with the audit scheduling data already sitting in the organisation, our training offers suddenly became timely and relevant. The result? Stronger uptake, happier clients, and less wasted effort.

A Lack of Bullet Holes

During World War II, Allied bombers returning from missions were riddled with bullet holes. Engineers studied the planes that made it back and carefully mapped where they were hit. The logic seemed obvious: reinforce the places with the most damage. More armor there would mean more planes surviving.

But one Bright Angler, Abraham Wald, a statistician with the U.S. military, saw things differently. Wald looked at the same bullet maps and noticed something others overlooked. "You're not seeing the whole picture," he pointed out. The engineers were only studying the planes that returned. They had no data on the ones that went down.

And that was the key. The bullet holes on the returning planes showed the places you could get hit and still make it back. Those were survivable hits. The places with no bullet holes? That's where the downed planes had been fatally struck.

Wald's recommendation flipped the logic on its head: don't reinforce the damaged areas, reinforce the untouched ones. The result was stronger, smarter armor and more planes surviving missions.

You see... the answer was there all along, staring them in the face but hidden in plane view. (I really hope you noticed my word play, quite proud of that one).

Fast-Food Groceries

Not that we particularly want to remember the year 2020, but when COVID lockdowns hit Sydney Australia, like much of the world, one of the scariest everyday tasks suddenly became grocery shopping. People were nervous about crowded aisles, empty shelves, and long queues. But at the same time, fast food drive-thrus remained open, quick, contact-minimized, and safe.

That's when McDonald's (or Maccas, as the Aussies call it) realized they had a hidden key. What do they already have in abundance? Buns from the burgers, milk from the coffees and eggs from their breakfast range. And what did households suddenly need most? Bread, milk and eggs.

So, McDonald's did something brilliantly simple: they sold staples through the drive-thru. No new stores, no new supply chains, just a bright angle on what was already there. Aussies could grab their Big Mac and their grocery basics without stepping into a supermarket.

It was a clever example of hidden value sitting right under their big red nose. Nice one Ronald.

Zebra-Cows

Not sure why you would, but if you've ever watched a cow for longer than a minute, you'll probably notice it constantly twitching its head, neck, and tail to shoo away flies, especially the biting ones.

All that twitching, known as *fly irritation*, might look trivial, but it drains energy and raises stress levels, both of which can nibble away at milk production. Farmers have tried all sorts of fixes: sprays, traps, even giant fans. But Japanese researchers found a hidden key hiding in a hide.

Whose hide? Zebras.

That's right, zebras suffer far fewer fly bites because their black-and-white stripes confuse the insects' visual sensors. So the researchers painted white stripes on their black cows, and it worked. Fly irritation dropped by 50 percent. With less energy wasted on twitching and tail-swishing, cows could graze more efficiently and turn that saved effort into a little extra milk.

Shuffling Keys

Have you ever wondered why your computer keyboard isn't laid out in alphabetical order? Well originally, they were. Some of the earliest typewriters experimented with an A-to-Z keyboard layout. It looked tidy on paper, but in practice it was a disaster, speedy typists would strike adjacent common letter pairs too fast, and the typebars would jam.

Christopher Sholes, working on the Remington typewriter, found a clever fix: scatter the most common letter pairs across the keyboard. The new QWERTY layout allowed typists to continue typing at speed but avoid striking two adjacent typebars. The hidden key was the layout. Interestingly, even though key jamming is no longer an issue, QWERTY was so widely familiar that keyboard layouts have remained the same ever since.

So, what's the lesson here? Well, remember to check your head for your reading glasses, ask your colleague what data they're already holding, and most of all, try reshuffling what's right in front of you. You might just uncover a hidden key that's been camouflaged, waiting to be found.

Chapter 3
Halving Problems

Big problems can feel impossible, until you cut them down to size. Sometimes ingenuity is nothing more than finding a way to make the problem smaller, simpler, or easier to manage. Half the trouble, half the stress.

Color-Coded

Not to keep banging on about my restaurant days, but I do have another simple bright angle I feel is worth sharing. It was so simple, so subtle, and yet it made such a difference to our customer service that I still think about it.

This was while working for a different restaurant chain, and the system worked like this: customers ordered at the counter, took a number on a stand, and sat down. Staff would then carry plates of food and drinks through the restaurant scanning table after table, looking for the matching number.

It was awkward to watch. Staff zig-zagging between tables, trays wobbling, food cooling, customers waiting. All because finding a table meant scanning the whole dining area every single time.

I decided to float an idea I had at one of our team chats, it was something so small it almost felt silly: we color-coded the table numbers. Evens in one color, odds in another. Suddenly the search was cut in half. Staff weren't scanning every stand anymore, they knew immediately which ones to ignore.

The effect was instant. Meals arrived hotter. Service was quicker. The staff looked less harried. And all because of a tweak so small it could be overlooked.

That's what I loved about it: ingenuity doesn't always mean solving everything. Sometimes it means quick-fixing sub elements to make the whole more manageable.

The Original Best Thing

Who doesn't love bread? Even gluten-free bread is adequately edible these days. I think you probably know where I'll be going with this one.... Yes, sliced bread. But how did it come about?

Bread had been around for thousands of years of course, but it was Otto Rohwedder who realized in the 1920s that the real hassle wasn't baking it, it was slicing it. At home, people hacked through loaves with knives, ending up with wonky slices, crumbs everywhere, and half the loaf squashed flat.

Rohwedder's bread slicing machine did the halving for them, perfectly even slices, ready to eat, pack, or toast. The convenience was so obvious that within a few years, the phrase "the best thing since sliced bread" had spread into everyday language.

Sliced bread itself became the benchmark against which all future innovations were judged. Talk about a breadwinner!

Dual Carriage Way

Another one I like that most people have probably used without noticing, is the reversible lane, sometimes called a tidal-flow lane.

These are the traffic lanes that change direction depending on the time of day: more lanes flowing into the city in the morning, then flipped to carry people back out in the evening.

Urban planners in Phoenix, Arizona, were doing this in the late 1970s, reporting a 30 percent drop in delays and a clear boost in average traffic speeds. But the idea goes back even further, Los Angeles was experimenting with movable lane markers as early as 1928. Since then, bridges, tunnels, and motorways all over the world, from New York to Shanghai, have adopted the trick.

Ok, so maybe not quite halving the problem of traffic congestion, but still a clever angle on how to tackle it.

Flushed with Options

Speaking of halving a problem, and I suspect not one you were expecting, you've probably noticed most modern toilets have two flush options: a full flush and a half flush. Well, turns out that was developed by Bruce Thompson and his team at Caroma who thought to themselves, surely there's no need to waste as much water simply for doing your business, especially in countries prone to drought.

They designed a cistern with two buttons. One flushed with half the amount of water as the other (for you know, let's say... less heavy waste).

It didn't reinvent plumbing, it wasn't supposed to, but it did shrink the daily drain on water simply by giving people a choice. The impact was enormous: households saved as much as 32,000 liters of water per year, and before long, dual flush systems became standard in building regulations.

Dark Bright

Here are some other witty ways clever people have been able to slice their problems. Farmers in hot, dry regions can save up to half their water just by irrigating at night, less sun, less evaporation. And in factories with automated assembly lines, some companies literally save millions on power bills by keeping the lights off. Robots don't need to see, the lights only come on when humans step in for checks or repairs.

...Poor robots, they don't even get a lunch break.

Chapter 4
Oddball to Obvious

Do you remember the early days of AirPods and hands-free earphones? People walking around talking to themselves looked a little daft, like they were arguing with invisible friends. Fast forward a few years and the script flipped. Now it's the people with corded earphones who feel judged, like primitive primates wrestling with a tangled ball of wires.

(Confession: I am one of those primates.)

This chapter is about bright angles that at first seemed peculiar, even laughable, but proved so effective they became the obvious way. And the first example might surprise you: the humble shopping trolley.

The Shopping Trolley

Back in the 1930s, shoppers carried baskets. Wire or wicker, heavy and awkward, they limited how much you could buy.

Sylvan Goldman, a supermarket owner, saw the problem and came up with what he thought was a simple fix: put the baskets on wheels, add a handle, and let people roll their groceries instead of carrying them.

It should have been an instant success. But when Goldman introduced the first trolleys, people thought they looked a little absurd. Men dismissed them as "baby carriages." Women said they made them look weak. No one wanted to be seen using one.

Undeterred, Goldman hired greeters and actors to wheel them around in his stores, making them look normal. Slowly, customers gave them a try. And once they did, the benefits were obvious: bigger shops, less effort, more comfort. Sales went up.

Skip to the present, and the shopping trolley has become so standard you don't even think about it.

The Spork

This next bright angle could have easily squeezed into the previous chapter on halving problems. After all, what is a spork if not a spoon and a fork cut in half and mashed together? A sort of

Frankenstein creation. But let's be honest, it fits better in this chapter. Why? Because it looks odd. A little awkward. The runt of the cutlery family.

The first patents for spoon–fork hybrids go back as far as the late 1800s. But for decades, the spork was more punchline than product. Too shallow to be a proper spoon, too stubby to be a serious fork. And yet, the spork found its place. Airlines loved it: one utensil that saved weight, space, and money. Prisons and schools adopted it because it was cheap and safe(r). Campers and fast-food chains embraced it for sheer convenience. Bit by bit, the oddball became obvious.

Today, the spork is widely accepted. It's found its confidence and now struts alongside its cutlery cousins, a proven utensil with its own niche strengths.

The Fosbury Flop

Before 1968, athlete high-jumpers all cleared the bar face-first or sideways. That was just how it was done. Then Dick Fosbury came along and did something that looked ridiculous: he ran up, twisted, and went over the bar backwards, landing flat on his back.

Crowds laughed. Peers tutted. Coaches muttered. To many, it looked like a mistake, not a technique. Even Fosbury admitted people thought he was "goofing around" in training. It was ungainly, unorthodox, very oddball-esque.

But then came the 1968 Mexico City Olympics. Fosbury stuck with his awkward-looking style, and against the odds, he won the gold medal. Overnight, the world's perception changed. The clumsy "flop" became a revelation.

Within just a few years, almost every elite high jumper had adopted his technique. Today, every record in the high jump has been set using the Fosbury Flop.

As for Fosbury himself? He went from the oddball kid with a funny jump to a sporting legend, inducted into the U.S. Olympic Hall of Fame and remembered as the man who literally turned his sport upside down.

The Flip-Turn

Staying in the world of sports, another bright angle that looked surprisingly peculiar at first is the flip turn in swimming.

We're all familiar with it now, and if you've ever managed to do one, you'll feel pretty cool gliding off the wall into a streamlined dive. But imagine competitive swimming before flip turns existed. The thought of tumbling head-first, at speed, and inches from the wall would never have crossed anyone's mind.

As it turns out, the modern flip turn, or tumble turn, was first used by Al Vande Weghe in 1934. Before that, swimmers would touch the wall with their hand, pivot, and push off. Functional, but clunky. Al's simple somersault changed everything. In one fluid motion, swimmers could touch, flip, and launch back down the pool, carrying momentum instead of losing it. It looked odd at first but it quickly became the gold standard.

So what's the takeaway from these examples? Well, for me it's this: if it looks a little strange today, it might just be tomorrow's standard.

Perhaps the very fact that it looks strange could even be a sign it's on the right track.

And if you don't want to take *my* word for it, take Albert Einstein's...

"If at first the idea is not absurd, then there is no hope for it." — Albert Einstein.

Ok Albert, that may be a tad too strong, but we get what you're saying.

Chapter 5
Happy Accidents

Not all bright angles are planned. Some stumble into existence by mistake, a failed attempt, an overlooked detail, or a lucky accident that turns out to be far more than what was intended.

Cowboy Pants

Ever thought about what cowboys would wear if it wasn't for Levi Strauss? Well of course not, that's just silly. But it is strange to imagine a world without denim jeans. And I bet you probably didn't know their very existence is a bit of an accident.

In the 1800s, Strauss, a Bavarian immigrant, travelled to California during the Gold Rush to sell goods to miners. Among his stock was a roll of heavy canvas, meant for tents and wagon covers. But there was a problem: the fabric wasn't waterproof and never really took off for its intended purpose.

Not willing to give up, Strauss then realized the miners had a different problem: their trousers wore out too quickly. So, he repurposed the canvas into durable work pants. They were stiff, but strong enough to last in the mines. Soon after, Strauss switched to an even sturdier cotton twill fabric imported from a town called Nîmes in France, "de Nîmes," or denim. And the rest is history. What began as failed tent fabric became the rugged uniform of miners, then cowboys, then the entire world.

The Non-Stick Glue

One of the most famous happy accidents came out of the labs at a company called 3M in the 1960s. A scientist named Spencer Silver (I know, cool name right!) was working on a project to create a super-strong adhesive. What he ended up with was the complete opposite: a glue so weak it barely stuck to anything. It didn't bond properly, it peeled off surfaces, and it had no obvious use. After all, who needs a glue that won't stick?

Enter Art Fry (again, what a name). Fry was a fellow 3M employee who also happened to sing in his church choir. He had a small but nagging problem: the little bits of paper he used to mark his hymnal pages kept falling out during rehearsals. He wanted a bookmark that stayed put but didn't damage the pages.

That's when he remembered the weak glue Silver had presented six years earlier. Just sticky enough to hold, but not so strong it would rip paper. Fry applied it to slips of paper and, to his delight, they worked perfectly.

Soon, colleagues were using them to jot reminders, stick notes on reports, and tag pages in documents. By the late 1970s, what began as a glue that "failed" at being strong became the Post-it Note, one of the most successful office products in history. Today, billions of them are sold every year.

A Fruitful Accident

If I asked you where Kiwifruits come from, you'd probably say New Zealand. And well, you wouldn't be wrong. But you wouldn't be technically right either. The fruit's true roots lie in China, where it was long known as the "Chinese gooseberry."

In the early 1900s, a New Zealand schoolteacher called Mary Fraser brought back a handful of seeds as a curiosity. Nobody expected much. But in New Zealand's soil and climate, the vines thrived, producing fruit that grew bigger, sweeter, and juicier than it ever had back in China. By the mid-century, growers realized they weren't just raising an exotic plant; they'd stumbled onto an export industry.

But exporting New Zealand–grown, bigger, sweeter, juicier Chinese gooseberries didn't really have that smooth marketing feel to it. That's when produce marketer Jack Turner suggested a rebrand. In 1959, he proposed naming it after New Zealand's national bird: the Kiwi. Suddenly it sounded fresh, simple, and unmistakably local. The new name stuck, and the rest is supermarket history. What began as a casual curiosity turned into a billion-dollar industry, a happy accident that proves sometimes it's not just about what you grow, but what you call it.

Dancing Goats

A tale of betrayal, ambition, secrecy, cover-ups, and ruthless diplomacy. A story that changed the world as we knew it. I'm talking, of course, about the history of coffee.

I know, it sounds like a trailer for a historical drama. But it's true. Coffee's rise is packed with smuggled seeds, political maneuvering in royal courts, cover-up campaigns to protect monopolies, and coffee houses that fueled revolutions. And yet, all that global drama can be traced back to a simple accident in Ethiopia.

According to legend, a goat herder named Kaldi noticed his goats dancing energetically after nibbling on red berries from a wild shrub. Curious, he tried them himself and felt the same rush. Hearing about it, monks from a local monastery gave them a try and had the bright angle to boil the beans and turn it into a drink.

That jittery hillside moment became the unlikely genesis for a drink that would spread across continents, reshape trade routes, and keep billions of us awake.

Happy accidents remind us that not all breakthroughs come from grand plans or meticulous strategies. Sometimes they tumble out of mistakes, missteps, or complete flukes, the kind of things you couldn't design on purpose if you tried.

Chapter 6
Magic Combos

Some bright angles don't come from inventing something entirely new. They come from taking two existing things, or even two parts of the same thing, and putting them together (or pulling them apart) in a way no one else thought to try. A clever pairing (including opposites), a little collision of ideas, and suddenly: hey presto, something fresh and brilliant exists.

Paper & Bees

Let's be honest: everyone hated the first generation of paper straws. They were well-intentioned, sure, goodbye plastic waste, hello eco-conscious sipping, but within minutes they turned into limp paper tubes, barely strong enough to stir your drink, let alone survive it. The bright angle came from a simple combo: paper + beeswax.

Paper brought the biodegradability, but it was far too absorbent. Beeswax, on the other hand, is naturally water-repellent, food-safe, and plentiful. By coating paper straws with a thin layer of beeswax, manufacturers gave them just enough protection to last through an entire drink without collapsing. The genius of the combo wasn't technological wizardry, it was restraint. No complex plastics, no hidden chemicals. Just a partnership between one flimsy biodegradable material and one water repellent food safe one, creating something functional, sustainable, and... well, not annoying. A small win for milkshake and bubble-tea lovers everywhere, and a much bigger one for turtles.

Fruits & Wallets

Ever thought of a pineapple as a handbag? Neither had I. But it turns out the pineapple is a bit of a magic combo in itself. For centuries, pineapples were grown for their fruit. The sweet yellow flesh went into juices, desserts, and fruit salads, (and pizzas for some strange reason), while the spiky green leaves were tossed away as waste. Tons of it, literally, rotting in fields. Then a Spanish PhD Student called Carmen Hijosa asked: What if the leaves weren't rubbish? What if they were a resource?

And she was absolutely right. The leaves happened to be packed with strong, flexible fibers. With the right processing, those fibers can be turned into a material she called Piñatex, a vegan leather alternative now used in shoes, handbags, and jackets. So, the same plant that gives you fruit for breakfast can also give you shoes to strut with.

It's not just clever, it's sustainable. Farmers earn more by selling what used to be waste. Brands get to shout about eco-friendly fashion. Consumers get guilt-free leather alternatives. One plant, two entirely different industries. That's the magic of combos, finding the hidden potential in what was already there.

Sound & Fire

We all know the usual ways to put out a fire, water, foam, blankets, or chemical extinguishers, but they all rely on having a ready supply of, well… those things.

What if there was another way? Sound good?

Well, it'd better sound good because researchers at Poland's Kielce University and engineering students at George Mason University discovered that by directing low-frequency sound waves at a flame you can disturb the flame's boundary layer, separate oxygen from fuel and snuff it out. They have even built prototypes of sound-wave fire extinguishers. So presumably it won't be long until they become viable accessible alternatives.

Safety Note – Please do not walk up to a fire and start playing bass guitar at it.

Fuel & Breath

In the 1940s, French naval officer Jacques Cousteau was chasing a dream, to breathe freely beneath the sea.

Only a few kilometers away, gas company engineer Émile Gagnan, invented a small pressure valve that regulated the flow of petrol allowing the flow to react on demand. This was a revelation in fuel-scarce wartime France.

When Cousteau laid eyes on it, he immediately realized it could do for air what it did for fuel. *"C'est magnifique!"* I'm totally sure he probably said.

He soon teamed up with Émile and adapted the design, creating the first self-contained underwater breathing system: the Aqua-Lung. A magic-combo that sparked a break-through into a whole new frontier.

Cloud & Heat

Here's a witty magic combo for you. Ready? Digital cloud data centers and district heating networks.

That's right, in Nordic cities such as Stockholm and Helsinki, the enormous heat produced by data centers (which was once simply vented away) is now harnessed by connecting those servers directly into the city's heating grid. The result? Nearby homes and offices stay warm through the winter. It's such a great example of discovering added value from an existing asset.

Origami & Safety

Folding paper into tiny cranes and swans doesn't sound like it has much to do with car safety. But here's the combo: origami + airbags.

The problem with airbags was storing them. They needed to expand in milliseconds to save lives but had to be packed away neatly inside steering wheels, dashboards, or side panels for years without anyone touching them. Early attempts worked in principle but were messy in practice: airbags would crease unpredictably, deploy unevenly, or simply take up too much space.

That's when engineers borrowed from an unlikely source: the ancient Japanese art of origami. Mathematicians and paper-folding experts (yes apparently that's a thing) had been developing algorithms to fold large, flat surfaces into compact, consistent shapes. By applying those same principles to the fabric of airbags, designers created folds that were tight, efficient, and guaranteed to deploy smoothly. It worked so well that origami-inspired folding is now used far beyond cars.

The space industry uses it to fold solar panels and telescope mirrors into rockets. Not bad for a childhood art of paper birds and flowers.

Some combos come from putting unlikely things together. Others come from looking at something familiar and realizing it has more than one trick up its sleeve. Either way, when worlds collide (or split apart), that's often when the magic happens.

Chapter 7
Forward Backward

I'll admit it: my top, absolute favorite bright angles are the low-tech ones. There's just something masterful about solving a big problem with an answer so basic you want to high-five it.

Take the old story of the "space pen." NASA, or so the legend goes, spent millions designing a pen that could write in zero gravity. The Russians? They just used pencils. (Not quite how it really happened, but still, a fun story to tell.)

And that's the point of this chapter: clever fixes that prove you don't always need cutting-edge tech to make a big difference. Sometimes the brightest angle comes not from going forward into complexity, but backward into simplicity.

Two Pots

Picture a rural village in northern Nigeria in the 1990s. Electricity was scarce, and farmers were losing much of their harvest before it ever reached the market. Tomatoes spoiled in days under the relentless heat. Food security was fragile.

Enter Mohamed Bah Abba, or MBA, as I like to call him, a schoolteacher who believed the solution didn't need wires, switches, or a power grid. His answer became known as the Zeer pot, or two-pot fridge.

The design couldn't have been simpler: take two clay pots, one slightly smaller than the other. Place the smaller one inside the larger, fill the gap with wet sand, and put your fruits and vegetables inside. As the water in the sand evaporates, it cools the inner pot, keeping the contents fresh for weeks instead of days. No electricity. No moving parts. Just clay, sand, and a little water.

The results were transformative. Tomatoes that used to last three days now lasted three weeks. Families saved food, farmers earned more, and communities gained resilience.

The Space Cup

Astronauts have long relied on straws and squeeze pouches to drink in zero gravity, because liquid doesn't politely sit at the bottom of a cup in space. Instead, it floats, blobs, and drifts away.

But there's a hidden down-side. On Earth, sipping coffee or tea is more than hydration, it's ritual, comfort, and smell. In space, sealed pouches mean no aromas rise to the nose, and without smell, taste is dulled. Coffee turns into brown water, soup into bland mush. That might sound small, but on long missions where morale is fragile, losing flavor is losing joy.

In 2008, astronaut Don Pettit decided to tackle the problem himself. He cut and folded plastic sheets into a sharp-angled cup, testing it on the International Space Station. What he discovered was elegantly simple: liquid naturally clings to surfaces through capillary action. By shaping the cup's edge into a narrow, curved channel, he created a pathway for the drink to flow straight to his lips. No gravity, no straw, just physics.

NASA and Portland State University engineers later refined Pettit's idea into the "space cup," which astronauts now use to sip coffee the way we do on Earth. And with that, the aromas return, flavor returns, and so does a little piece of home.

Timber Satellites

Here's another example from space, because well, why not? When you think "space technology," you probably picture titanium alloys, carbon fiber, or some futuristic composite with a name like Brightanium Anglium. (Scientists, feel free to use... who knows, might be a bright marketing angle.)

But in 2024, a team of researchers at Kyoto University and Sumitomo Forestry unveiled something that sounded more like a high-school project: a wooden satellite.

The idea was as simple as it was clever. Traditional satellites leave behind dangerous debris when they burn up on re-entry, scattering metal fragments into orbit, space junk that clutters Earth's skies and threatens other spacecraft. Wood, on the other hand, burns away completely when it re-enters Earth's atmosphere.

And here's the kicker: in space, wood doesn't rot or degrade. Mold needs oxygen. Without it, wood just sits there, stable, flexible and intact, the perfect low-tech material for a high-tech frontier.

Standing

Ok back down to Earth now and how about a bright angle that's so low tech it has no tech at all!

This one is literally just about standing up. Huh? I hear you exclaim. Well, if you've ever sat through a long, meandering meeting, you'll know the pain. People settle into their chairs, the conversation drifts, and before you know it, an hour's gone, and nothing's been decided.

Then came the simplest intervention ever: take away the chairs. The stand-up meeting was born. By keeping everyone on their feet, meetings shrank from an hour to fifteen minutes. People stayed focused, cut the waffle, and got back to work.

The idea had floated around workplaces for decades, but it was the software world that really turned it into a staple. From there it spread beyond coding teams into companies everywhere.

So you see, low-tech doesn't have to mean low impact. Sometimes the way forward is to go backward, to embrace the simple, humble and unassuming solutions.

Chapter 8
Animal Rescue

Nature has had a much longer head start than us when it comes to problem-solving. Millions of years of trial and error, evolution's giant R&D department, quietly refining designs while we were still figuring out how to bang stones together to make fire. It's no surprise that some of our cleverest bright angles come straight from the animal kingdom.

Fast Skin

It's not often people can say they were saved *by* a shark instead of *from* a shark. Well... "saved" might be a bit of an overstatement, but for Speedo in the late 1990s, sharks did come to the rescue... kind of.

The company was facing increasingly stiff competition from rivals like Arena and Adidas. Everyone was chasing sponsorships and innovation, and Speedo needed something to maintain its dominance in the pool. Their answer? Borrow from an apex species, specifically, the shark.

Shark skin isn't smooth, it's covered in tiny, tooth-like ridges called denticles. These break up water flow and reduce drag, letting sharks slip through the ocean with remarkable efficiency.

Speedo's R&D team, Aqualab, decided to copy it. Working with scientists at Flinders University and fluid dynamics experts, they developed the Fastskin suit, a swimsuit with fabrics textured to mimic shark skin. The results were spectacular. Records fell, medals piled up, and by the 2008 Beijing Olympics, nearly every gold medal swimmer was wrapped in shark-inspired fabric.

An Ant-trawling Insight

Humans like to think we invented logistics, but ants have been running delivery systems for millions of years.

When ants leave the nest in search of food, they don't just wander aimlessly. Each one lays down a trail of pheromones. If another ant finds food, it reinforces that trail on its way back. Soon the strongest path is the one with the most pheromone "upvotes," and the colony naturally converges on the most efficient route.

No maps, no managers, no GPS, just chemical breadcrumbs and teamwork.

Scientists studying these patterns realized they were looking at a living algorithm. Researchers translated ant behavior into what became known as "ant colony optimization." Suddenly, delivery companies, data networks, and airline schedulers had a new model for solving one of their trickiest problems: how to get from A to B as efficiently as possible when thousands of routes are competing.

Today, the paths traced by FedEx trucks, Uber drivers, and even packets of data racing across the internet owe something to the humble ant. So thank you ants for rescuing us humans from our own inefficiencies.

A Gripping Solution

Well, I don't mean "gripping" as in a page-turning novel, I mean it literally. This one's about grip.

Geckos, those little lizards you sometimes see darting up walls in tropical countries, have a party trick that seems to defy physics. They can run straight up vertical walls and even hang upside-down on glass, as if gravity forgot to apply to them. For centuries, people guessed at how they did it. Tiny suction cups? Some kind of sticky excretion? Not quite.

Biologist Kellar Autumn put a gecko's foot under a powerful microscope and discovered the truth: each toe was covered in millions of microscopic hairs, called setae. These split into hundreds of even finer tips, so small they interact directly with the molecules of the wall through van der Waals forces, weak attractions that, when multiplied millions of times, are strong enough to hold the lizard's entire body weight.

Best of all, the grip can be broken instantly just by changing the angle of the foot.

Engineers couldn't resist. In 2003, physicist Andre Geim (yes, the same scientist who once famously levitated a frog with magnets, and later won the Nobel Prize for graphene, but I'm sure you already knew that) and colleagues at the Max Planck Institute in Stuttgart developed the first gecko tape. By mimicking the gecko's microscopic hairs with arrays of polymers and carbon nanotubes, they created a dry adhesive that clings tightly to glass, metal, and even ceilings, yet peels off cleanly and can be reused again and again.

And here's where the "rescue" part comes in. Traditional adhesives don't work in zero gravity, but gecko tape does.

NASA has been experimenting with it for space robots and tools, because a material that can stick without glue, without residue, and without gravity is a lifesaver in orbit.

Ok so maybe not likely to change my life or your life but still, pretty cool.

The Mold Template

Now this one is really weird. Imagine a solution inspired by an animal that doesn't even have a brain. Yep, no joke.

Meet the slime mold, a yellow, pulsating blob that spends its life creeping across forest floors in search of food. It looks like something you'd scrape off your shoe, not a master planner. But when researchers in Japan scattered oat flakes on a map in the shape of Tokyo and let a slime mold loose, something unexpected happened.

Over a few days, the mold crept outward, sending out thin veins to connect the food sources. (Aren't you glad this isn't a picture book.) When the researchers compared the mold's network with the actual Tokyo rail map, the resemblance was uncanny. Even more surprising: the slime mold's design used fewer connections while still maintaining efficiency. In other words, a brainless blob had templated a rail network that could be cheaper and more resilient.

So what's the rescue angle with this one? Well, let's just say Tokyo Rail's financial forecasters might have seen it that way.

There are countless more fascinating examples of biomimicry out there. If, like me, you enjoy those types of bright angles I recommend you look up how the flippers of humpback whales inspired a clever redesign of wind turbines, or how the kingfisher bird's beak inspired bullet trains' acousto-dynamic shape.

Chapter 9
Riveting Pivoting

I am not a martial artist, but I've watched enough martial arts movies to learn one thing: sometimes the smartest move is the unexpected one. And in business and life, it's the same. Sometimes the smartest move isn't doubling down on what you're already doing, it's recognizing that the current way isn't working. When the path ahead is blocked, the brighter angle isn't to push harder, it's to pivot.

Some pivots *change how you play the game.* Others *change the game you play.*

This chapter is about those kinds of bright angles: the riveting pivots that can seem counter-intuitive in the moment but end up redefining success. And I'll start with two of my own, not quite Bruce-Lee-level obviously, but a reminder that even small pivots can swing the result.

Prime Time

Back when I was managing a training academy, I sat in on a sales team meeting where everyone looked frustrated. The complaint was the same:

"No one's picking up, no one's getting back to us."

At first glance, it sounded like the market just wasn't interested. But as I listened, I realized something: they weren't struggling with prospects, they were struggling with timing.

Most of the calls and emails were going out when it suited the team: convenient slots around their own meetings, admin tasks, and coffee breaks. Nobody was stopping to ask, "When's the best time for the customer?" So, I raised the question: "What time of day are people actually most likely to pick up?"

Cue silence. It hadn't really been thought about. All they could tell me was what time *not* to call. "Well then, from that can't you deduce the best time?" I spoke. "Put yourself in their shoes, what time would you be more inclined to answer a call or email?"

That simple nudge triggered a positive conversation that quickly led to a clear split: maybe-prime-time vs maybe-not-prime-time slots. Embarrassingly, it turned out the regular sales team meeting was smack bang in the middle of a maybe-prime-time slot. And that of course prompted the sales team leader to rethink their whole schedule. Meetings were moved to maybe-not-prime slots, admin work was shifted too, and the prime slots were freed up and dedicated purely to sales calls and emails.

You may be thinking, well, that's so obvious. I mean, it's not like its rocket surgery. But hey, sometimes you've got to challenge even the most basic assumptions. And the effect was instant. Response rates jumped, conversions improved, and morale lifted. Nothing about the product changed, nothing about the pitch changed, the pivot was the reorganized approach.

From Gut Feel to Smart Bids

Later, when I was working as an innovation analyst for a global design and construction firm, I saw a similar issue at a bigger scale. The sales team spent a huge amount of time preparing tenders, but the decision to bid or not was mostly gut feel. Whether we chased an opportunity or not depended more on hunches than on data. Clearly, a brighter angle was needed.

The fix wasn't glamorous. We simply built a rough and ready scoring calculator using Microsoft Excel. For each tender, we inputted the client's criteria and scored ourselves, and our suspected competitors, against them. A little desktop research filled in the rest. Suddenly we could see which bids were worth chasing, where to double down on our strengths, and which weaknesses or competitor advantages we'd need to neutralize. The result? Less time wasted on long-shot tenders and more energy devoted to the ones we were likely to win. A small pivot in approach, but one that shifted the odds firmly in our favor.

The JIT Pivot

Have you ever heard of a little Japanese company called Toyoda Automatic Loom Works? No? Well, I'm sure you've heard of its offshoot car division, Toyota. These days it's one of the most recognizable brands in the world and for decades has been the top-selling car manufacturer globally. But back in the mid-20th century, it wasn't obvious that Toyota would become a world leader. At the time, the rule of manufacturing was simple: bigger batches = cheaper production. Henry Ford had shown the world the power of economies of scale, build vast quantities, stockpile them high, and unit cost drops. Factories churned, warehouses filled, and that was the accepted way to play.

Toyota looked at that playbook and thought: what if we pivoted instead? Instead of economies of scale, they went for economies of flow. Build only what's needed, when it's needed. Deliver parts to the line just in time. Let workers stop the line if there's a fault instead of pushing defects downstream.

Their pivot became known as Just-in-Time (JIT). At first, outsiders thought it was madness. Too risky. But it worked. Inventory costs dropped, waste shrank, quality improved, and Toyota quietly grew into a global powerhouse. By the 1980s, Toyota wasn't just surviving, it was leading. And slowly, the rest of the world had to admit that their pivot paid off big time. Today, lean manufacturing and JIT principles are everywhere.

From Game to Workplace Platform

Today Slack is so woven into modern offices it feels like it's always been there. But Slack's origins are surprisingly quirky: it came out of a failed online game called Glitch.

Glitch was colorful, eccentric, and much-loved by its small fan base. But it never broke into the mainstream. The development team eventually had to admit the game wasn't working and pulled the plug.

But buried inside the project was a tool they'd built for themselves: a chat system to keep the developers organized, share files, and track progress. Unlike the game, the chat tool worked beautifully. It was fast, fun, and made team communication smoother than email.

The team realized the real treasure wasn't the game at all, it was this chat platform. They pivoted, polished it, and launched it to the world as Slack. Within a few years, millions of workers were using it daily. The quirky game faded into history, but its by-product became a billion-dollar industry standard.

The Customer Service Revolution
If you're old enough to remember the world before the year 2000... yes, I know, the music was better. (Is that even up for debate?) Anyway, one thing you might not remember so fondly: customer service surveys. (Bet you weren't expecting that).

Back then, most companies measured success in the bluntest of ways: cut costs, increase sales, profits go up. Simple. Except... not so simple. Cutting costs worked for a while, but eventually sales dipped. When sales dipped, profits followed. Cue more cost-cutting. It became the corporate sport of the day.

You've probably heard the famous story of the airline that supposedly saved thousands by removing a single olive from every passenger salad. Cute? Sure. But while executives were patting themselves on the back for shaving off an olive, they weren't asking the bigger question: *were customers actually happier?*

So companies turned to surveys. Long, painful surveys. A million and one questions asking customers to rate every tiny detail of their experience. The result? Fewer people completed them, and the answers they did get were muddy and inconclusive.

Then along came a hero of sorts: Fred Reichheld. (Not exactly a superhero name, but hey, function over form right?) In 2003, while at Bain & Company, Reichheld published a now-famous article in the *Harvard Business Review* titled *"The One Number You Need to Grow."* His suggestion was spit-takingly simple: instead of interrogating customers with a hundred questions, just ask one that really mattered:

"On a scale of 0 to 10, how likely are you to recommend us to a friend or colleague?"

From that single question came the Net Promoter Score (NPS), a clean, powerful way to separate promoters (loyal advocates) from detractors (the grumblers who might actively dissuade others) and to measure how well a company was inspiring loyalty.

When Fred published his article, he probably didn't expect to launch a movement. But that's exactly what happened. It was an industry pivot. Instead of obsessing over cost-cutting, companies like General Electric, Intuit, and Enterprise Rent-A-Car shifted focus toward cultivating loyal "promoters."

Suddenly, growth wasn't about squeezing margins, it was about creating customers who would *sell for you* through word-of-mouth. Net Promoter Score became the language of boardrooms, investor decks, and quarterly reviews. Whether you love it or roll your eyes at it, NPS changed the way entire industries thought about customer experience.

Nintendo and Nintendon't

You may be surprised to learn that Nintendo originally made handcrafted playing cards. Over the years they've pivoted like a pinball machine, taxis, instant rice, even vacuum cleaners. (I wonder if that was to clean up the rice.) None of these stuck until they turned to electronic toys and video games, where they finally found their true calling.

Sometimes it takes more than one pivot to land in the right game.

Chapter 10
Re-Angling

People love to say, *"If it ain't broke, don't fix it."* But here's the thing: "not broken" doesn't mean "couldn't be better." Bright angles often appear when someone refuses to leave "good enough" alone, and decides to give the familiar a re- angle.

The Pasta That Spelled Fun

For decades, canned pasta in tomato sauce was about as exciting as a cement block: functional, and forgettable. The kind of meal that plodded along unchanged, more survival than celebration.

Then in 1969, Heinz pulled a simple but brilliant trick. No new sauce, no fancy ingredients, just a change of shape. They reshaped the noodles into letters of the alphabet. Suddenly dinner wasn't just dinner. Kids could spell their names in sauce. Parents could pass it off as educational. A dull tin of pasta had turned into playtime.

The recipe hadn't changed a bit. But the *experience* was completely different. And that was enough to reboot a tired old staple into Alphabetti Spaghetti, a product that became a household name and a reminder that sometimes form really can top function.

Side fact:
Some gloriously bored researchers once worked out how many cans of Alphabetti Spaghetti it would take to spell out the entire text of *The Lord of the Rings*. The answer? 8,795 cans. Proof, if ever needed, that humanity always finds time for the important questions.

This Vacuum Sucks!

There was a time when every vacuum cleaner looked the same: a box on wheels, a bag to collect the dust, and a cord to trip over. Functional, yes. Inspiring? Not really.

Then along came a now famous bright angler: James Dyson. He grew frustrated when his vacuum lost suction mid-clean. Instead of blaming the carpet, he blamed the design. The bag, he realized, was the bottleneck, clogging, reducing airflow, and dulling performance. So, he borrowed an idea from industrial sawmills that used cyclonic separation to remove dust from the air. Five thousand prototypes later, Dyson unveiled a bagless vacuum. No clogging, no loss of suction, and suddenly something that had "worked fine" for decades looked embarrassingly outdated.

Dyson didn't invent the vacuum. He simply refused to accept "good enough." By re-angling the design, he transformed a boring household chore into a billion-dollar brand.

Bottling the Obvious

Decades ago, the thought of paying for water in bottles would have seemed laughable. Water was free, abundant, and ordinary. Why would anyone buy it? But clever marketing reangled it: Perrier made it chic in the 1970s, Evian sold "purity from the Alps," Fiji Water went exotic, and suddenly bottled water wasn't just a commodity, it was a *Blue Ocean Strategy* in action. A whole new market was created where none had existed before. What was once free became premium, branded, and desirable.

Now the same thing is starting to happen with air. In air-polluted cities from Beijing to Delhi, fresh air isn't taken for granted, it's a luxury.

Canadian startup Vitality Air began shipping canisters of Rocky Mountain air to China, where a single bottle could sell for the price of a decent lunch. In the UK, a company called Aethaer started bottling "bespoke British countryside air" for high-end buyers. Swiss firms capture Alpine breezes. There are even "luxury" versions packaged in glass decanters, like fine wine.

At first, it sounds absurd, paying for something as basic as a breath. But so did bottled water, until it didn't. These are the kinds of re-angling that open new "oceans" of opportunity.

I know, I'm also starting to look around and think, what else could be rebooted, re-angled, or even bottled? Do you think there'll ever be a way to drink a book?!...

Ok, ok, back to reality.

Anyway, on the subject of water bottles and re-angling, guess what?... a company called FreeWater is attempting to flip the model once more. Instead of charging customers, they give the bottles away for free. The trick? Each bottle is covered in ads. The brands pay; the drinker doesn't.

A Master Re-Angler

If Dyson reimagined the vacuum and Heinz reimagined pasta, Richard Branson reimagined entire industries. He was less an inventor, more a *Re-Angler-in-Chief*.

His playbook was simple: spot a market that had gone stale, and flip it. Record shops in the 1970s were intimidating and overpriced, so Virgin Records made them cheap, relaxed, and fun. Airlines in the 1980s were stuffy and joyless, so Virgin Atlantic added entertainment, ice cream, and personality. Mobile networks in the 1990s tied customers into rigid contracts, so Virgin Mobile broke the mold with pay-as-you-go freedom.

Branson's genius wasn't about technology. It was about business models. He took what already existed, shook off the dust, and re-angled the value proposition. Virgin didn't so much invent as *intervene,* showing that sometimes the brightest angle isn't a breakthrough, but a shake- up.

Rest At Your Peril

We all know the danger of 'resting on your laurels.' History is littered with examples, here are two that span centuries.

China perfected porcelain centuries ago, so perfect, in fact, they never felt the need to push further with glass. Meanwhile, in Europe, glass kept evolving into microscopes, telescopes, and lenses, that quietly set the stage for a scientific revolution. One civilization rested on its strengths, the other angled forward. But complacency is contagious. The West had its own "good enough" moment in the 20th century. Plastic credit and debit cards worked fine, so why change? In China, though, payments quickly skipped to mobile phones propelling it to the front of financial innovation.

The lesson? Comfort can be a trap. Whether it's porcelain or plastic, resting on what works today can leave you watching someone else sprint past tomorrow.

Chapter 11
Curve Busting

In the great words of Monty Python: *"And now for something completely different..."*

Why? Because this chapter is all about bright angles that bust curves, so I figured I should bust the curve of my own book while I'm at it. Practice what you preach, right?

You see, all the chapters so far have followed a similar format: essentially a bunch of examples *Venn Diagramically* aligned to a theme. But this time I'm breaking my own pattern.

Instead of examples, here you'll find quiz questions. (Don't worry no studying required, it's just for a bit of fun.)

And so, without further ado,

(drum roll please...).

Welcome to the Curve Busters Quiz!

Question 1
Which curve busting invention was inspired by a dog walk and some plant burrs?
A)   Velcro
B)   Nylon
C)   Fiber Optics
D)   Zippers

Question 2
Which type of code inspired Joe Woodland to invent the Barcode?
A)   Enigma Code
B)   Morse Code
C)   Binary Code
D)   Davinci Code

Question 3
Who was the inventor of the remote control?
A)   Hedy Lamarr
B)   Thomas Edison
C)   Nikola Tesla
D)   Matilda Wormwood

Question 4
Which civilization first pioneered freeze-drying as a deliberate method of food preservation?
A)   The Egyptians
B)   The Incas
C)   The Vikings
D)   The Smurfs

Question 5
Which of the below curve busting inventions were invented by the Romans?
A)   Aqueducts
B)   Central heating
C)   Sewers
D)   None of the above

Question 6
Which of these curve busting inventions were directly attributed to and inspired by the popular television series Star Trek?
A)   Flip Phones
B)   Tasers
C)   Automatic Sliding Doors
D)   All the Above

Note: Quiz answers are on the next page

Quiz Answers:

Q1 = A) Velcro
Swiss engineer George de Mestral noticed burrs clinging stubbornly to his dog's fur after a walk. Curious, he looked under a microscope and saw tiny hooks that latched onto loops of fabric and hair. A decade later, "Velcro" (from "velvet" + "crochet") was born.

Q2 = B) Morse Code
Joe Woodland, while sitting on a Miami beach, drew dots and dashes in the sand, inspired by Morse code. He stretched them vertically, making lines of varying thickness, and the idea for the barcode was hatched.

Q3 = C) Nikola Tesla
Not Edison, not Hedy Lamarr (though she did help invent Wi-Fi), and sadly not Matilda Wormwood, the Roald Dahl character who could move objects with her mind. In 1898, Tesla wowed crowds at Madison Square Garden with a radio- controlled boat, the world's first remote control. Many thought it was magic or trickery, but it was really a *bright angle* decades ahead of its time.

Q4 = B) The Incas

High in the Andes, the Incas left potatoes out overnight to freeze, then let the sun and thin air draw out the moisture. The result was *chuño,* rock-hard, feather-light spuds that could last for years. It kept armies fed, villages resilient, and trade routes open long before freezers or fridges.

Q5 = D) None of the above

Yes, the Romans were clever, but aqueducts, sewers, and central heating all predated them. The Romans were brilliant at scaling and refining infrastructure, but they didn't invent those particular marvels. A nice reminder: sometimes the bright angle is improving what already exists.

Q6 = D) All the above

Flip phones, tasers, and automatic sliding doors all drew inspiration from Star Trek. Engineers, inventors, and sci-fi geeks alike took cues from the show's vision of the future. Proof that fiction can spark fact, and that sometimes the brightest angle is imagining boldly.

Well, I hope you found that quiz fun.

Now though, I want to let you in on another cheeky reason why I decided to mix it up a little. You see back when I used to run train-the-trainer courses, I would teach my trainers about accelerated learning techniques and how to bust what is known as the Ebbinghaus Forgetting Curve.

Hermann Ebbinghaus was a psychologist who studied memory (or at least I think that's what he studied...). His experiments showed that about 70% of what people learn is forgotten within 48 hours. Depressing, right? But the curve isn't fixed, you can dent it. One of the best ways? Make learning playful, surprising, or fun.

And that I guess is one key takeaway from this chapter, not whether or not you got all answers correct, (although if you did, major kudos!). But that making things a little more fun makes learning more seamless. Which is a good bright angle way to help others retain information you'd like them to.

And while we're still on curves, here's one more to chew on: the curve of history itself.

Historians often talk about the Industrial Revolutions, those seismic shifts that changed how humans lived, worked, and dreamed. Each one was, at heart, a giant curve-buster:

I. The First Industrial Revolution swapped muscle power for steam, a clunky water-pump technology that ended up powering trains, ships, and factories.

II. The Second used electricity and assembly lines to bust the curve of handcraft, making goods faster and cheaper than anyone thought possible.

III. The Third pulled computers into offices and homes, busting the curve of human clerical work.

IV. And the Fourth, the one we're living now, is fueled by AI, biotech, and networks, busting curves not just in industries but in knowledge and even biology.

None of these looked inevitable at the time. Steam engines started as mine pumps. Early computers filled whole rooms. Yet each became the dent that busted the curve and leaped the world forward into a new age.

I wonder what the fifth industrial revolution will involve?...

How good would teleportation be?, Think about it... Instant takeaway delivery, zero traffic, kids beamed straight to school. Or even a quick trip to Mount Everest without the... you know... strenuous climbing part.

We simply need to figure out how to defy physics, I'm sure the rest is easy-peasy.

Chapter 12
Wrong Angles

Bright angles aren't always right angles. Some ideas flop. Others fizzle. A few crash and burn so spectacularly they end up in business school textbooks.

But wrong angles still matter. They remind us that innovation is messy, timing is tricky, and even the smartest people misjudge.

So let's take a look at a few favorites from the hall of fame (or should I say hall of shame) of wrong angles.

Too Off

The Chevrolet car company's Nova compact car sold well in the US but sold less well in Latin America, why? Well had they done their local research properly they would have realized that "no va" literally translates as "doesn't go." A name fail that became marketing folklore.

Too Far

What do you associate Harley-Davidson with? Burly bikes, leather jackets, the smell of petrol. What you probably don't think of is... perfume. Well, in the 1990s, Harley tried to stretch its brand into fragrance. The problem was, no one wanted to *smell* like a Harley. They wanted to ride one. The mismatch was too far from what the brand stood for. Unsurprisingly, it bombed.

Too Much

And now how about this one. You may not remember or recognize the name and for good reason. In 2016, Juicero, the $400 Wi-Fi-connected juicer that could only squeeze proprietary juice packs, became a Silicon Valley punchline. Investors poured in millions before someone discovered you could get the same result just squeezing the packs by hand.

Sometimes the wrong angle is just an over-engineered answer to a non-existent problem.

Too Soon

Launched in 2013, Google Glass promised a future of augmented reality right in your line of sight.

A head-mounted display with voice commands and apps, basically a smartphone for your face. The problem? Society wasn't ready. People were uncomfortable with hidden cameras, the battery life was terrible, and the price tag was sky-high. The product flopped.

But here's the kicker: today AR headsets, smart glasses, and mixed reality are making their comeback. Google Glass wasn't necessarily a bad idea, it was just too soon.

Too Careful

Not every wrong angle comes from doing the wrong thing. Sometimes it's from *not* doing a thing.

Back when I managed restaurants, delivery apps were starting to take off. Competitors were jumping in, signing up with platforms that promised customers meals on their couches with just a few taps. We hesitated. Our thinking was simple: we wanted to protect quality. Food was meant to be plated, served hot, and presented just right, not crammed into plastic containers and handed to a courier with a backpack.

So we stalled. We told ourselves, surely customers would think our food wasn't as good if their impression of it is from the delivered version. But customers clearly thought differently. While we guarded standards, rivals were racking up orders. Their food might have been colder and soggier, but it was *there*, in people's homes, fast and easy. And that mattered more.

By the time we finally joined the delivery game, the damage was done. Competitors had captured loyalty, and it took us a long time to claw back the market share we'd lost.

The lesson? Sometimes the biggest wrong angle isn't a bad idea you chased, it's the good idea you didn't.

The general point isn't to smirk and laugh (well, maybe a little). It's to remember that wrong angles don't mean game over. They're just the messy side of ingenuity, reminders that timing, fit, and even hesitation all matter as much as the idea itself.

A wrong angle today can still be a bright angle tomorrow... if you're willing to learn from it and try again.

Chapter 13
Sparking

Okay, so, after all these stories, you might be wondering: "Yes, fun examples... but so what? How can I use these?"

Look, I'll level with you: like most things in life, there's no silver bullet answer. I can't claim to know or have possession of some magic dust that will instantly make bright angles appear. If I did, I'd like to think I'd now be slurping a mojito while sunbathing on the helicopter pad of my supersonic yacht.

But what I can offer are my idea-nerd observations. After years of watching teams, experiments, and oddball ideas up close, I've noticed certain conditions that tilt the odds in favor of bright angles showing up. Think of them as sparks: not guaranteed fire, but a way to get the flame going.

So what are they? Well, the first three are somewhat obvious, I'm sure you could have deduced yourself:

1. Constraints

Give people less, and they'll often come up with more. Think of the Zeer pot in rural Nigeria: no electricity, no fridges, just two clay pots, wet sand, and evaporation. That tiny constraint unlocked a way to keep food fresh for weeks.

Give it a try:
- Cut your next project in half, half the slides, half the budget, half the time.
- Run a brainstorm where ideas must fit a Post-it note, or be explained with three emojis.
- Cook dinner without salt, sugar, or one of your "can't live without" ingredients.

Constraints don't just block options, they force sharper angles.

2. Cross-pollination

Many bright angles come not from digging deeper, but from crossing boundaries.

IDEO, the famous design firm, has built its reputation not on lone geniuses but on curated mixes: an anthropologist, a toy designer, and an engineer might be thrown at the same problem. Casting directors do the same with film ensembles and sports coaches know it too: a fiery motivator balanced with a calm strategist can turn a locker room around.

In other words, the act of bringing the right people into the room is itself a bright angle. You don't always need to be the smartest person in the meeting, you just need to make sure the right brains are blended together.

But cross-pollination isn't just about who you mix into the room, it's also about what you mix into your own head. Many bright angles happen when you step outside your lane, borrow a lens from somewhere unexpected, and then bring it back.

Give it a try:
- Ask a friend in a totally different field to weigh in on your challenge.
- Read a book or watch a documentary outside your usual taste, then ask: "What if this applied to my work or my situation?"
- Host a mixed brainstorm where everyone brings an idea stolen from another industry.

Sometimes the best fertilizer for ideas is pollen blown in from elsewhere.

3. Thumping Assumptions

Often the cleverest move is simply asking: "What if the opposite were true?" Toyota did this with Just-in-Time. Everyone else stockpiled, Toyota didn't. The result? Lean manufacturing.

Give it a try:

- Flip your next meeting, start with decisions, end with updates.
- Write down three assumptions about your situation. Then flip them: what if the opposite were true?
- Ask: "What if we stopped doing this altogether?"

It may sound absurd. But, as Einstein said, absurdity is often the first sign of brilliance.

4. Permission to Play

Bright angles don't usually show up when you're grinding at your desk. They appear when people feel they can joke around, engage in both shoptalk and non-shoptalk chats, toss out oddball ideas, and step back.

Sometimes permission is implicit, but people don't realize it. So best to communicate it.

I know, you might be worried about setting a precedence you'll regret, but I can tell you, it does have huge success potential.

Some organizations engineer this. One that I worked for shuffled team's office seating location every six months, a hassle at first, but a silo-buster in practice. Another had showers and locker rooms, and lunchtime jogs became idea factories.

I'm willing to admit, some of my own best bright angles have arrived not in a workshop, but in the shower. Weird? Maybe. But I bet you've got your own unlikely best thinking spot: half-asleep in bed, mid-jog, staring at the ocean, or listening to Vivaldi, Enya or your favorite heavy metal techno hip hop band.

Give it a try:
- Kick off your next meeting with a playful icebreaker: "invent a useless gadget in 30 seconds", and see how much easier real ideas flow afterward.
- Swap a standard desk huddle for a walking meeting, or host it somewhere unexpected (park bench, café, stairwell). Shifts in environment often spark shifts in thought.

- Invite everyone to pitch the worst, silliest, or most impractical idea they can. Nine times out of ten, something useful hides inside the nonsense.

5. The Other Kind of Brightness

Bright doesn't just mean clever. It also means hopeful. Some of the most inspiring bright angles weren't born from a neat trick or quirky pivot, but from the sheer brightness of optimism.

Take *The Ocean Cleanup*. Boyan Slat was a teenager when he announced his plan to tackle the clumpy continent of plastic floating in the Pacific. Scientists were skeptical, headlines were dismissive, but he pressed on. Today his organization is actively pulling tons of waste from rivers and oceans. The angle wasn't just the tech, it was the refusal to believe the problem was too big to try.

Or look at Wikipedia. When it began, the idea that strangers across the world would freely volunteer their time to write an encyclopedia sounded ludicrous. Encyclopedias were supposed to be written by credentialed experts behind closed doors. And yet, the optimism that "people will contribute if given the chance" built the largest knowledge project in history.

The sheer belief that problems can be solved, that people will help, that progress is worth trying for is the optimism that can make bright angles possible.

Give it a try:
- Next time you're tackling a challenge, pause and list *three good things* that could come out of solving it. Even small wins reframe the effort as worthwhile.
- At the start of a project, ask: *"What's the best that could happen?"* It doesn't mean you'll get there, but it pulls your thinking toward possibility instead of fear.
- Make it a team ritual to share one story a week of someone solving a "too big" problem. Optimism is contagious when you feed it.

And look, I know some of the examples in this book involved big corporations, labs, and PhDs. But I hope you also noticed that many came from people who simply permitted themselves to play a little, step back, and rethink. They didn't need to be rocket surgeons. They just needed to be curious, willing, and open to looking at a problem from a slightly different angle. And really, anyone can do that.

That's why I keep saying: bright angles can come from anywhere, and anyone, and even anything (remember the yellow goop mold example). And if you're wondering how to put all of this into practice, feel free to follow the Bright Angler's Field Guide only a couple pages away.

Well, I hope at the very least this book has helped you hitch a ride on the idea-nerd wagon. Obviously, there are many more examples I could have added, and exactly infinity plus one more out there waiting to be found, activated, even generated.

Oh, and one more thing. Here's another way to help others in your sphere spark their own bright angles... let them borrow this book. Or better yet, gift them a copy. (Hey! who said that? ...Hehehe).

So here's my invitation: give yourself permission to play. And when you discover your bright angles, share them. And keep looking out for more. You never know, they might sow seeds for even greater ones.

And on that note, thank you for reading. I bid you good luck, and happy bright angling.

Over to You

Though this is the end of the book's chapters, bright angles don't stop here. They never do. And now this is where you come in.

Bright angles aren't fussy. They pop up in offices, kitchens, classrooms, jungles, space stations, and yes, even in your bathroom. All it takes is someone to notice the potential twist.

So keep your eyes open, your curiosity switched on, and your optimism dialed up. Keep looking sideways at problems everyone else stares at head-on. And who knows, maybe the next great bright angle the world talks about will be yours.

Appendix
The Bright Angler's Field Guide

Table of Contents

When I Have No Ideas   92
*For those staring at a blank page, an empty
whiteboard, or the dreaded "any ideas?"
silence in a meeting.*

When I Have an Idea   94
*For when you've got a spark but don't know
if it's genius, garbage, or both.*

When I'm Facing a Tricky Problem   96
*For when you feel stuck, the knot is too
tight, or the system too messy.*

When I Want to Inspire My Team   98
*For leaders, managers, or anyone trying to
spark creativity in others.*

When I Want to Avoid Wrong Angles   100
For staying out of traps, fads, or dead ends.

**When I Want to Build a Bright Angling
Culture**   102
*For senior leaders shaping organizations,
not just projects.*

When I Have
No Ideas

For those staring at a blank page, an empty whiteboard, or the dreaded "any ideas?" silence in a meeting.

☐ **Shift the lens**
Don't ask "What's my idea?" Ask "How else could I look at a problem?" Pretend you're the customer, the competitor, or even a kid/alien seeing the problem for the first time. Sketch the challenge as a map, rename the parts, or redraw it upside down.
- o *See Chapter 1: Shifting Views — Harry Beck's Tube map didn't change the trains, just the way people saw the network.*

☐ **Cut it smaller**
Big blank canvases are overwhelming. Halve the scope. Ask: *What's the one-slide version? The half-budget version?*
- o Run a "half it" workshop: take a challenge and brainstorm what you'd do with half the staff, half the money, or half the time. You'll be surprised how often leaner = sharper.
- o *See Chapter 2: Halving Problems — sliced bread and dual flush toilets proved that halving isn't losing, it's liberating.*

❏ Borrow from nature

Nature has already solved billions of problems. When stuck, ask: *How would ants organize this? How would a gecko grip it? How would a shark streamline it?*

- o Flip through *Chapter 6: Animal Rescue* — from gecko inspired tape to slime mold rail maps, biology is a library of ready-made bright angles.

❏ Lean into accidents

What went wrong lately? That failed experiment, clumsy error, or misstep might be your seed.

- o Try the "happy accident audit": list five recent mistakes and ask, *"What else could this be useful for?"*
- o *See Chapter 4: Happy Accidents* — a weak glue became Post-it Notes; tent fabric became jeans.

❏ Stay bright

Optimism isn't just "good vibes." Expecting that an answer exists literally makes your brain search harder and notice more.

- o Write three statements of belief: *"There is a solution. I will spot it. Something small can spark it."*
- o *See Chapter 13: Sparking* — optimism was the secret fuel behind Wikipedia and The Ocean Cleanup.

When I Have an Idea

For when you've got a spark but don't know if it's genius, garbage, or both.

☐ **Test the oddball**
Strange is often a signal. Ask: *If this looks silly, what unseen advantage might it carry?*
- o Run a "weirdness workshop": list what seems impractical or laughable about your idea — then brainstorm what hidden strengths those quirks could hide.
- o *See Chapter 3: Oddball to Obvious —* the Fosbury Flop looked foolish until it became the gold standard.

☐ **Pilot tiny**
Don't try to build the big thing yet. What's the 30-minute version? The paper prototype? The conversation test?
- o Try "one-hour prototyping": make something scrappy that captures the essence, then test with a friendly critic.
- o *See Chapter 8: Forward Backward —* astronaut Don Pettit made the first space cup with folded plastic sheets.

☐ **Pair it up**

Mash your idea with another to see what magic happens.

- o Try "combo roulette": put your idea on one sticky note, then draw random nouns from a hat (pineapple, skateboard, opera) and force yourself to imagine the mashup.
- o *See Chapter 5: Magic Combos —* origami + airbags saved lives; pineapple leaves + fashion became Piñatex.

☐ **Re-angle it**

Could the same idea hit harder in a different form or audience?

- o Ask: *What if this was for kids? Seniors? A rival's customers? A different industry?*
- o *See Chapter 10: Re-Angling —* Dyson didn't invent vacuums, he just re-angled the design.

☐ **Sell the bright future**

Don't pitch features; paint futures. Say: *"Imagine how your day looks once this works…"*

- o Use "future postcards": ask your team to write a postcard from 3 years in the future describing the impact of the idea.
- o *See Chapter 13: Sparking —* optimism makes ideas magnetic.

When I'm Facing a Tricky Problem

For when you feel stuck, the knot is too tight, or the system too messy.

☐ **Halve the headache**
Break the beast into smaller bits. Ask: *Which part could I solve this week?*
- o Use "sticky note surgery": split every problem into at least three smaller ones. Solve the easiest first.
- o *See Chapter 2: Halving Problems —* reversible traffic lanes and color-coded table numbers worked because someone shrank the scope.

☐ **Flip the assumption**
Write down your three biggest assumptions. Then flip them.
- o Example: *"We must reduce cost" → "What if we increased cost?"* The absurdity often reveals overlooked truths.
- o *See Chapter 7: Riveting Pivoting*

☐ **Stay buoyant**
Keep energy alive by writing down three reasons why this problem *is* solvable.
- o *See Chapter 13: Sparking —* belief helps you spot options you'd otherwise miss.

☐ Look for hidden keys

The answer may already be in your world. Check the obvious places you've ignored.

- o Run a "what's in the cupboard?" audit: data, past reports, old prototypes, unused assets.
- o *See Chapter 9: Hidden Keys* — Abraham Wald realized the missing bullet holes were the key.

☐ Go backward

Don't overcomplicate. Ask: *What's the simplest, lowest-tech way?*

- o Try the "Stone Age test": solve it with nothing digital.
- o *See Chapter 8: Forward Backward* — two clay pots became fridges, stand-up meetings cut waffle.

☐ Find the human angle

Complexity becomes clearer when reframed as one person's problem.

- o Write a mini story: *"Maria is frustrated because..."* Then solve for Maria, not the whole system.
- o *See Chapter 9: Hidden Keys*

When I Want to Inspire My Team

For leaders, managers, or anyone trying to spark creativity in others.

☐ **Set playful limits**
Don't say "think outside the box." Give a smaller box.
   ○ Run a "tweetstorm brainstorm": every idea must fit in 280 characters.
   ○ *See Chapter 13: Sparking* — constraints sharpened the Zeer pot and many others.

☐ **Celebrate accidents**
Make mistakes part of the mythology.
   ○ Run "Failure Fridays" where people share their flops and what they taught.
   ○ *See Chapter 4: Happy Accidents* — Post-it Notes and denim jeans were born from failures.

☐ **Tell oddball stories**
Keep a stash of bright angle anecdotes and drop them into meetings.
   ○ *See Chapter 3: Oddball to Obvious* — the spork is proof that odd can become obvious.

❏ Mix the minds

Cross-pollinate: bring together the unusual mix.

- ○ Try "guest stars": invite a non-obvious colleague or even a customer into the room.
- ○ *See Chapter 13: Sparking* — IDEO swears by mixing anthropologists, toy designers, and engineers.

❏ Make optimism visible

Teams take their emotional cue from leaders. End meetings with one positive statement of confidence.

- ○ *See Chapter 13: The Other Kind of Brightness* — optimism itself can be the spark.

When I Want to Avoid Wrong Angles

For staying out of traps, fads, or dead ends.

☐ **Don't stretch too far**
Ask: *Does this fit who we are?*
   o *See Chapter 12: Wrong Angles* — Harley-Davidson perfume didn't pass the smell test.

☐ **Solve real problems**
Always confirm someone is asking for it.
   o *See Chapter 12: Wrong Angles* — Juicero solved nothing that hands couldn't.

☐ **Watch the window**
Hesitation is its own failure.
   o *See Chapter 12: Wrong Angles* — restaurants who delayed delivery apps lost ground fast.

☐ **Learn forward**
Every failure is tuition. Document wrong angles and pivot from them.
   o *See Chapter 7: Riveting Pivoting.*

☐ **Beware the shiny**
Don't chase novelty for its own sake. Ask what changes if the hype fades.

☐ **Keep the core steady**
Innovate around your strengths, not away from them. If the angle erodes your base, it's probably wrong.
   - ○ See Chapter 4: Odd to Obvious — Fosbury flopped into success because it built on the *core* of high jump, not away from it.

When I Want to
Build a Bright Angling Culture

For leaders shaping organizations, not just projects.

☐ **Give permission to play**
State explicitly: *"Wild ideas welcome."* Reinforce it by rewarding experiments, even failed ones.
  ○ *See Chapter 13: Sparking – Permission to Play.*

☐ **Mix the disciplines**
Form squads across silos. Rotate team members every few months.
  ○ *See Chapter 13: Sparking — Cross-pollination.*

☐ **Anchor to optimism**
Be visibly confident that solutions will emerge.
  ○ *See Chapter 13: The Other Kind of Brightness.*

☐ **Design the system**
Build rituals that embed creativity: *"Bright Angle Days,"* stand-ups, walking meetings, rotating desks.
  ○ *See Chapter 8: Forward Backward.*

☐ **Anchor to optimism**
Shape a culture where teams deliver the
everyday fixes *and* dare to chase long shots.
Celebrate both.

    o   Use a reel of your organization's past
        bright angles to remind people that
        today's impossible often becomes
        tomorrow's obvious.

Quirky Quotes

Lastly, I thought I'd throw in some quotes from famous idea-nerds, many of which have inspired me or at the very least, made me chuckle.

"I have not failed. I've just found 10,000 ways that won't work." — Thomas Edison

"The best way to have a good idea is to have lots of ideas." — Linus Pauling

"If you obey all the rules, you miss all the fun." — Katharine Hepburn

"Discovery consists of seeing what everybody has seen and thinking what nobody has thought." — Albert Szent-Györgyi

"If I had asked people what they wanted, they would have said faster horses." — Henry Ford

"When you change the way you look at things, the things you look at change."— Wayne Dyer

"You can't use up creativity. The more you use, the more you have." — Maya Angelou

"Even nothing still contains a thing." — Me (I just made it up! I know, so lame and not sure what it means, but hey, why not give it a go right?)

Dedications

Before I close, I want to thank my parents, for giving me the perfect mix of freedom and guidance, curiosity without pressure, and the belief that even silly ideas were worth voicing.

To my sister, my earliest sounding board as well as family, thank you for always listening (and for the occasional eye-roll, which was just as valuable).

To the many friends, colleagues, bosses, and mentors, thank you for the guidance, nudges, and challenges that sharpened my thinking

But this book, truly, I dedicate to my darling wife, and to our two wonderful children. My wife, who somehow keeps me tethered to reality when I start to drift too far, and who does it with wit sharper than my own. And my son and daughter, who pepper me daily with curly questions from every angle, reminding me that curiosity is both endless and endlessly humbling.

And finally, a special mention to a very witty writer, my grandmother. I'd like to think she'd enjoy reading this book, and perhaps even claim a few bright angles of her own.

Author Bio

Daniel Alexander Maher was born in France, raised in Ireland, and now calls Australia home. He has travelled five continents, speaks four languages-ish, and once memorized every capital city, just to see if he could.

With a career spanning economics, management, and innovation, Daniel has led teams across hospitality, education, corporate, and public sectors, while mentoring entrepreneurs along the way. For the past eight years he has specialized in innovation, helping organizations find new ways forward. A lifelong explorer of ideas, he is fascinated by history, sport, space, comedy and gadgetry. *Bright Angles* is his first published book.

Free Space for Notes....

... Extra Notes...

...Hair-Brained Schemes...

...Moon-Shot Ideas...

... Eureka Moments ...

... and Doodles.